anythink

D0609386

ZOO CLUES

My Body Is Striped and Leafy

by Jessica Rudolph

Consultants:
Christopher Kuhar, PhD
Executive Director
Cleveland Metroparks Zoo
Cleveland, Ohio

Kimberly Brenneman, PhD
National Institute for Early Education Research
Rutgers University
New Brunswick, New Jersey

BEARPORT
PUBLISHING

New York, New York

Credits

Cover, © Alex Mustard/naturepl.com; 4–5, © Winkler, A./picture alliance/Arco Images G/Newscom; 6–7, © D.R. Schrichte/SeaPics.com; 8–9, © Astargirl/ iStockphoto; 10–11, © Terry Evans/Dreamstime.com; 12–13, © Mark Conlin/Alamy; 14–15, © Alex Mustard/naturepl.com; 16–17, © Krzysztof Wiktor/Shutterstock; 18–19, © Alex Mustard/naturepl.com; 20–21, © Alex Mustard/naturepl.com; 22, © Alex Mustard/naturepl.com; 23, © Satish Arikkath/Alamy; 24, © gracious tiger/ Shutterstock.

Publisher: Kenn Goin
Creative Director: Spencer Brinker
Design: Debrah Kaiser
Photo Researcher: We Research Pictures, LLC

Library of Congress Cataloging-in-Publication Data

Rudolph, Jessica.
  My body is striped and leafy / by Jessica Rudolph.
     pages cm. — (Zoo clues)
  Includes bibliographical references and index.
  Audience: Ages 5–8.
  ISBN-13: 978-1-62724-112-0 (library binding)
  ISBN-10: 1-62724-112-4 (library binding)
  1. Leafy seadragon—Juvenile literature. I. Title.
QL638.S9R83 2014
597'.679—dc23
                                    2013036948

For more information, write to Bearport Publishing Company, Inc., 45 West 21st Street, Suite 3B, New York, New York 10010. Printed in the United States of America.

10 9 8 7 6 5 4 3 2 1

Contents

What Am I?

Look at my body.

It is striped.

My eyes have white marks around them.

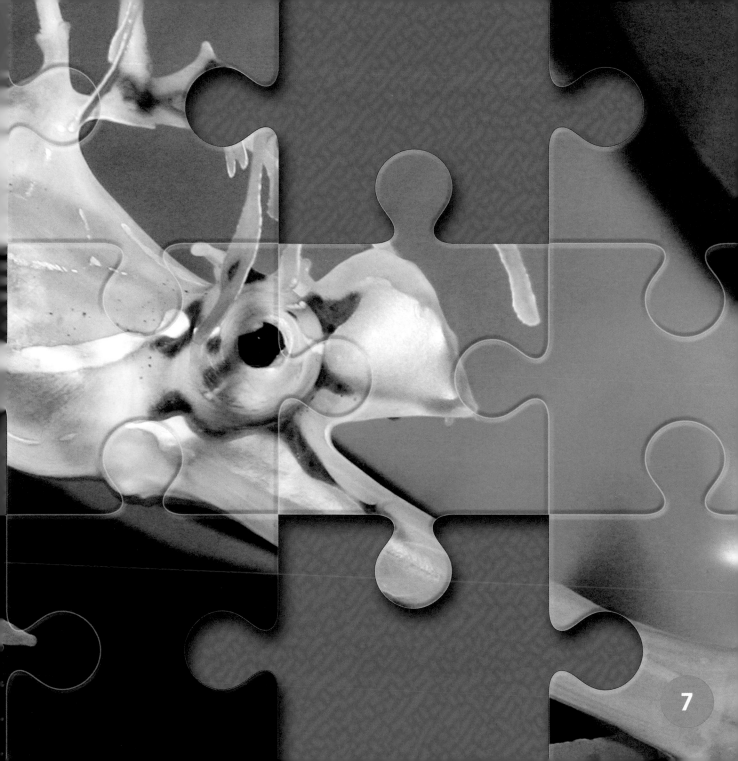

My body is curvy.

8

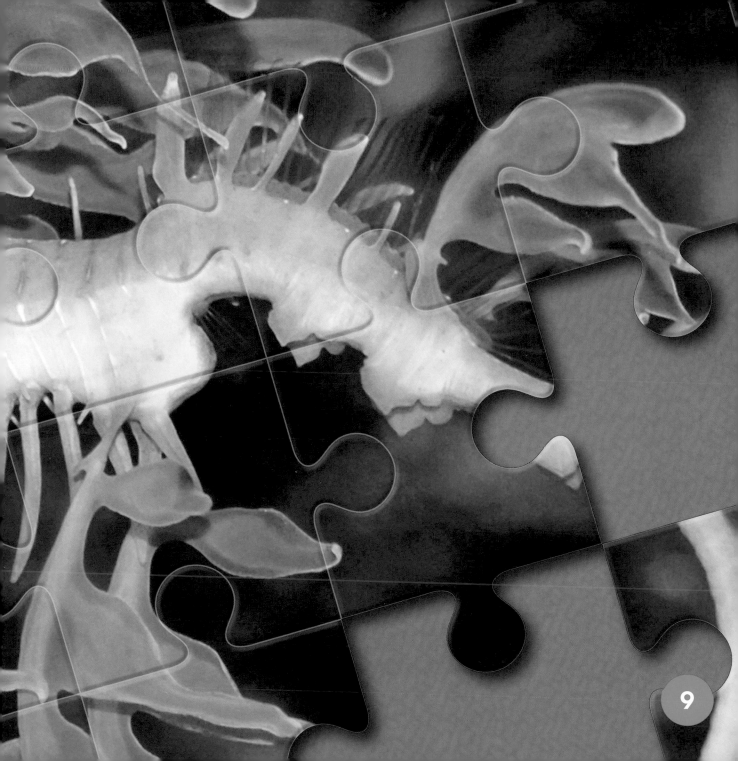

My tail is long
and thin.

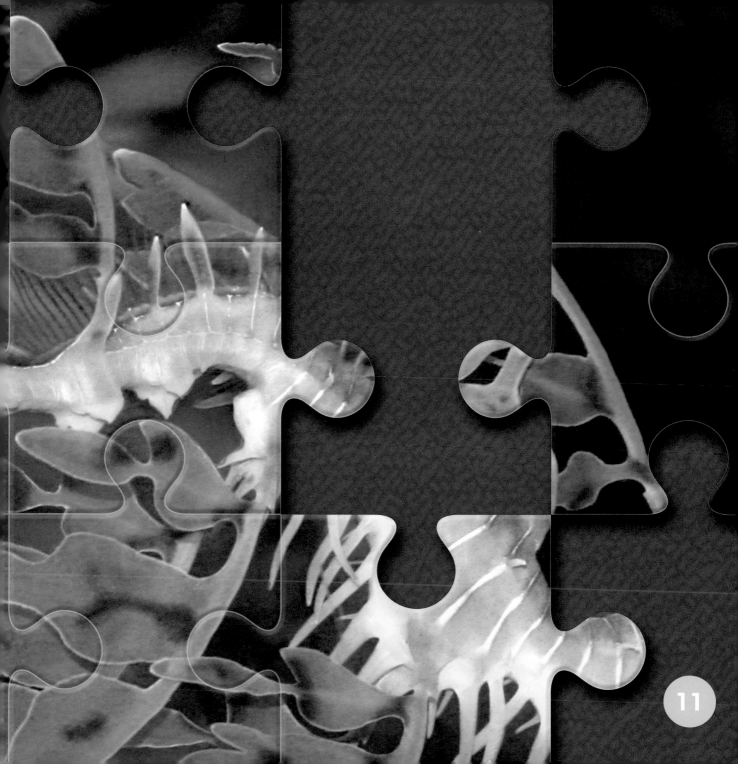

I have sharp spines on my sides.

13

My mouth is
shaped like a trumpet.

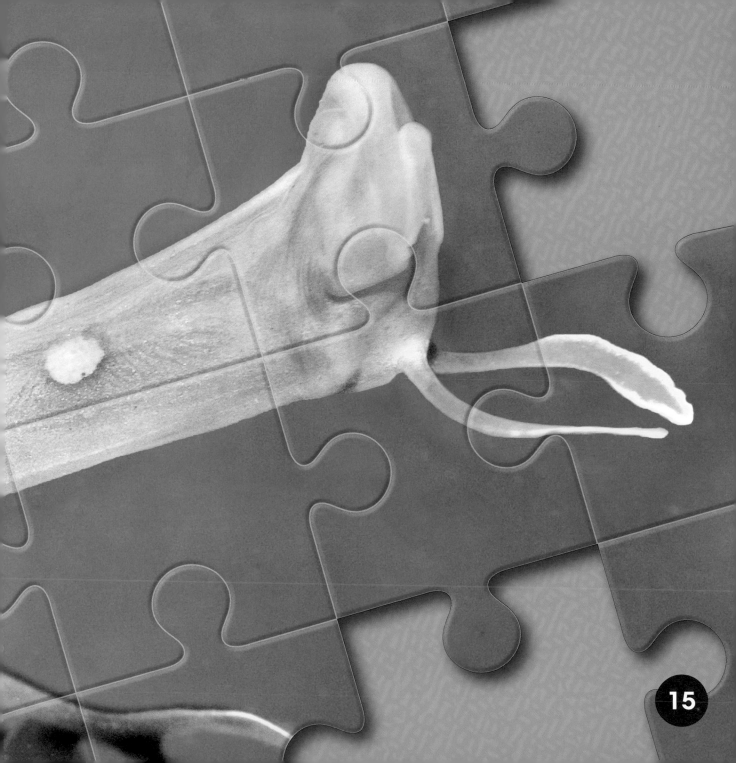

Parts of my body look like leaves.

17

What am I?

18

Let's find out!

I am a leafy
sea dragon!

Leafy sea dragons are fish that are related to sea horses. Like all fish, they use gills to breathe. They also lay eggs instead of giving birth to live young.

More Leafy Sea Dragon Facts

Food:	Tiny sea creatures called plankton
Size:	14 inches (35.6 cm) long, including the tail
Life Span:	About 5 to 10 years in the wild
Cool Fact:	The leaf-like body parts of the sea dragon help it to blend in with floating seaweed. This protects the sea dragon from other animals that want to eat it.

Adult Leafy
Sea Dragon Size

Where Do I Live?

Leafy sea dragons live in the ocean near Australia. They swim in shallow waters close to the coast.

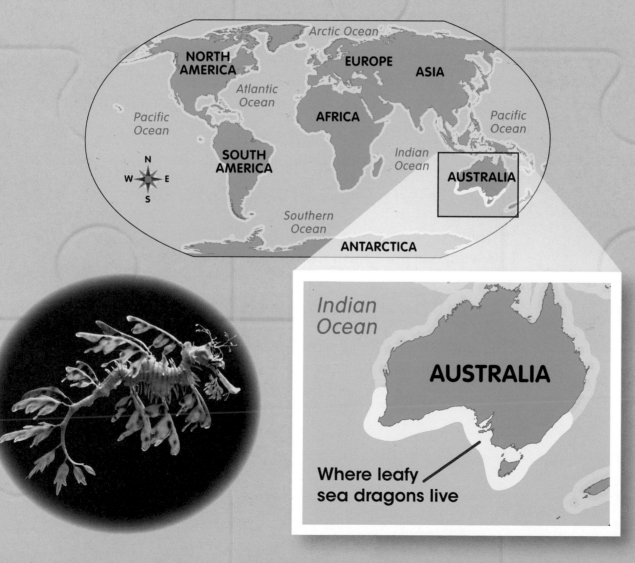

Where leafy sea dragons live

Index

Read More

Bredeson, Carmen. *Leafy Sea Dragons and Other Weird Sea Creatures (I Like Weird Animals!).* Berkeley Heights, NJ: Enslow (2010).

Schach, David. *Sea Dragons (Blastoff! Readers: Oceans Alive).* Minneapolis, MN: Bellwether Media (2007).

Learn More Online

To learn more about leafy sea dragons, visit **www.bearportpublishing.com/ZooClues**

About the Author

Jessica Rudolph lives in Connecticut. She has edited and written many books about history, science, and nature for children.